BEHIND THE SCENES
BIOGRAPHIES

WHAT YOU NEVER KNEW ABOUT

>>>———————————————<<<

PATRICK

MAHOMES

by Martha E. H. Rustad

CAPSTONE PRESS
a capstone imprint

Published by Spark, an imprint of Capstone
1710 Roe Crest Drive, North Mankato, Minnesota 56003
capstonepub.com

Library of Congress Cataloging-in-Publication Data
Names: Rustad, Martha E. H. (Martha Elizabeth Hillman), 1975- author.
Title: What you never knew about Patrick Mahomes / by Martha E.H. Rustad.
Description: North Mankato, Minnesota : Spark, an imprint of Capstone, 2022.
| Series: Behind the Scenes Biographies | Includes bibliographical references. |
Audience: Ages 9-11 years | Audience: Grades 4-6 | Summary: "Patrick Mahomes
has risen to fame as a superstar NFL quarterback. But what happens when he is not
on the gridiron? High-interest details and bold photos of his fascinating life will
enthrall reluctant and struggling readers, while carefully leveled text will leave them
feeling confident"— Provided by publisher.
Identifiers: LCCN 2021059237 (print) | LCCN 2021059238 (ebook) | ISBN
9781666356854 (hardcover) | ISBN 9781669040156 (paperback) | ISBN
9781666356861 (pdf) | ISBN 9781666356885 (kindle edition)
Subjects: LCSH: Mahomes, Patrick, 1995- —Juvenile literature. | Quarterbacks
(Football)—United States—Biography—Juvenile literature. | African American
football players—United States—Biography—Juvenile literature. | Kansas City
Chiefs (Football team)—History—Juvenile literature.
Classification: LCC GV939.M284 R87 2022 (print) | LCC GV939.M284 (ebook) |
DDC 796.33092 [B]—dc23/eng/20220604
LC record available at https://lccn.loc.gov/2021059237
LC ebook record available at https://lccn.loc.gov/2021059238

Editorial Credits
Editor: Erika L. Shores; Designer: Heidi Thompson; Media Researchers:
Jo Miller and Pam Mitsakos; Production Specialist: Tori Abraham

Image Credits
Associated Press: AP Photo/File, 14, John Sleezer/The Kansas City Star via AP, 25;
Getty Images: Christian Petersen/Staff, 22, Kansas City Star, 4, Kevin Winter/Staff,
10, Peter Aiken, 18; Newscom: TNS/David Santiago, 9; Shutterstock: Barre Kelley,
27, BearFotos, 21, Bochkarev Photography, 7 (bottom), creativestockexchange, 19
(top), Dan Thornberg, 16 (top), dean bertoncelj, 6, FocusStocker, 17, Jamie Lamor
Thompson, Cover, 20, 26, Jeff Bukowski, 13, JIANG HONGYAN, 28 (inset), Jiri
Hera, 19 (bottom), jjaf, 11 (right), Khalifa Illustrations, 11 (left), Macrovector, 7 (top),
Michael C. Gray, 28, New Africa, 24, Ranju sushi, 26 (inset), RoidRanger, 29, Sean
bedeck, 16 (bottom)

37892020519364

Printed in the United States   5840

TABLE OF CONTENTS

Words in **bold** are in the glossary.

TOUCHDOWN!

Patrick Mahomes throws the football down the field. He tosses some balls to nearby teammates. Other **passes** are nearly as long as the field. The ball is caught. It's a touchdown!

Mahomes plays in the NFL for the Kansas City Chiefs. But did you know he almost played pro baseball? What other facts about him might amaze you? Let's find out.

PAT STATS

Fans love the way Patrick Mahomes plays and wins. Think you know everything about him? Check your skills.

1. How fast can he throw a football?

2. Which number was on his college jersey?

3. True or False: He puts ketchup on Thanksgiving turkey.

4. How many Super Bowls has he won?

5. What is his middle name?

1. 62 miles (99.8 kilometers) per hour **2.** 5 **3.** true **4.** one **5.** Lavon

The most important stat for Mahomes is 50. He threw that many touchdowns in the 2018–19 season. He tied Tom Brady's record. Only Peyton Manning, with 55, has thrown more in a season.

Mahomes also threw more than 5,000 yards in one season. He is the only quarterback (QB) to throw that many yards in college and as a pro.

FACT

Patrick's arms are 33.25 inches (84.5 centimeters) long.

WINNING
ALL THE TIME

Mahomes's first NFL season was one of the best ever for a QB. And each year after, the Chiefs have made the playoffs with him on the team.

Mahomes led the team to the Super Bowl in 2020. They beat the San Francisco 49ers by a score of 31–20.

Patrick Mahomes puts the *P* and *M* in MVP. In 2018, he was named Most Valuable Player (MVP) in the whole NFL. He also was the MVP of the Super Bowl in 2020.

FACT

In 2019, Patrick won an ESPY award. It is given to the best NFL player.

2018 MVP

13

ALL THE
SPORTS

Patrick's father, Pat Mahomes

Football isn't the only sport Mahomes loves. He grew up around baseball. His dad played pro baseball for six teams.

In high school, Mahomes played baseball, basketball, and football. He played baseball and football in college.

FACT
Patrick grew up in Texas. He went to Texas Tech University.

The Tigers **drafted** Mahomes when he was 19. They wanted him to play baseball in Detroit. But he decided to stay in college. He chose to play only football.

The Chiefs aren't the only team he cares about though. He is part owner of the Kansas City Royals baseball team. He also is part owner of the Sporting Kansas City soccer team.

SHOW ME
THE MONEY

What would you do with $503 million? You could spend $2,011 every day. It would last you 685 years. That is how much money Mahomes earns. He is one of the highest-paid athletes in the world.

Mahomes has to work every single day. Work out that is! He lifts weights and runs. He throws a lot of footballs too.

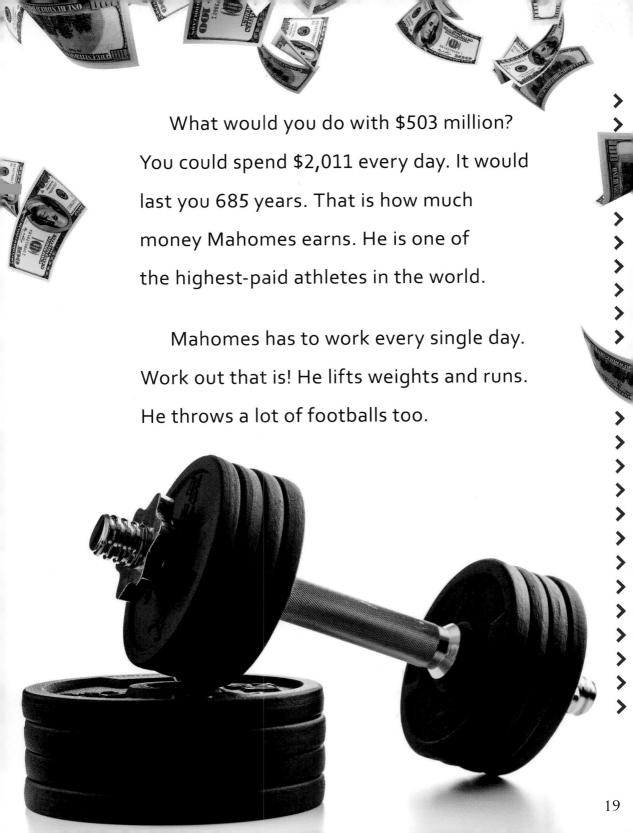

HOME, SWEET
MAHOMES

FACT

Patrick and Brittany met in high school.

Mahomes owns a ranch-style house in Kansas City. He lives there with his wife, Brittany Matthews, and their daughter, Sterling. His dogs, Silver and Steel, play in the yard.

One room is just for shoes. The room has special shelves and lights. Mahomes wants to be able to see all his kicks. He has about 180 pairs of sneakers!

BIG TIME
NAME

^ ^

^ ^

What else do people call the K.C. QB? Some of his friends call him Pat. His mom always calls him Patrick. As a kid, his dad called him Showtime. Some teammates call him Magic Mahomes. His full name is Patrick Lavon Mahomes II.

FACT

When Patrick throws the ball, he often sticks out his tongue.

---

^ ^

15 AND THE
MAHOMIES

Mahomes gives back. He started 15 and the Mahomies. The group visits kids in schools and hospitals. It helps kids pay for school lunches.

Mahomes also helps kids play. He gives money to youth football teams. 15 and the Mahomies rebuilt Martin Luther King Jr. Park in Kansas City. Kids of all ages and abilities play there.

FAVE
FOODS

Mahomes missed Whataburger when he moved to Kansas City. It is his favorite fast-food place. He missed it so much that he's helping open several Whataburgers in the Kansas City area.

Patrick even has his own cereal! Mahomes Magic Crunch is sweet and flaky.

Mahomes loves ketchup. He puts it on almost everything. Mac and cheese? Yep! Steak? Yep! He even does ads to sell his favorite brand of ketchup.

Kansas City is known for its **barbecue**.
One sandwich is Mahomes's favorite.
The Z-Man has beef, cheese, and onion
rings. It's as terrific as one of his terrific
touchdown passes!

Glossary

barbecue (BAR-buh-kyoo)—meat that is cooked or smoked over a fire

draft (DRAFT)—a way for pro teams to pick players

jersey (JUR-see)—a shirt worn by a team member; each player has a different number

pass (PASS)—to throw the ball to a teammate

Read More

Corso, Phil. *Patrick Mahomes.* New York: PowerKids Press, 2021.

Levit, Joe. *Meet Patrick Mahomes*. Minneapolis: Lerner, 2022.

St. Sauver, Dennis. *Patrick Mahomes: Superstar Quarterback.* Minneapolis: Abdo, 2020.

Internet Sites

Patrick Mahomes
chiefs.com/team/players-roster/patrick-mahomes/

Patrick Mahomes Facts for Kids
kids.kiddle.co/Patrick_Mahomes

Patrick Mahomes' Top 25 Throws (So Far)
video.link/w/HjHAc

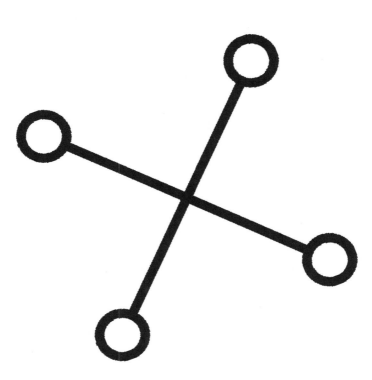

Index

About the Author

Martha E. H. Rustad is the author of more than 300 nonfiction children's books, on topics ranging from baby ducks to black holes to ancient Babylon. She lives with her family in Brainerd, Minnesota.

B
MAHOMES **DATE DUE** 9/24

FOLLETT